ONE PATH TO PEACE IN PALESTINE

ONE PATH TO PEACE IN PALESTINE

T. Hans Olson

Primix Publishing
East Brunswick Office Evolution
1 Tower Center Boulevard, Ste 1510
East Brunswick, NJ 08816
www.primixpublishing.com
Phone: 1-800-538-5788

© 2025 T. Hans Olson. All rights reserved.

No part of this book may be reproduced, stored in a retrieval system, or transmitted by any means without the written permission of the author.

Published by Primix Publishing: 08/13/2025

ISBN: 979-8-89194-533-3(sc)
ISBN: 979-8-89194-534-0(e)

Library of Congress Control Number: 2025915095

Any people depicted in stock imagery provided by iStock are models, and such images are being used for illustrative purposes only.

Certain stock imagery © iStock.

Because of the dynamic nature of the Internet, any web addresses or links contained in this book may have changed since publication and may no longer be valid. The views expressed in this work are solely those of the author and do not necessarily reflect the views of the publisher, and the publisher hereby disclaims any responsibility for them.

Contents

Introduction And Back-story vii
Six Principles of Peace............................1
A Letter...12
    Prime Minister Ariel Sharon
    Office of the Prime Minister

    President Yasser Arafat
    The Palestine Liberation Organization
    Negotiations Affairs Department

Essay Art... 10 Point Peace Proposal

    A Maze 18
    An Attractive Alternative 20
    Back To The Basics 22
    Evaluating Outside Insights Effectively 26
    Voluntarily Vulnerable......................28
    Impartial Inspiration 30
    Resolving Change............................32
    The Big Picture.............................34
    The Carrot And The Stick 36
    The Peaceful Prolonged Process 38

Essay Art... Learning From Palestine

    The Beauty Of Change 41
    Should We Change?..........................43

How To Change... 45
Every Cell Has Memory..... 48

Essay Art... Change and Inspirations

As Easy AS ABC...
    The "Artful" Approach To Change.........51
As Easy As ABC...
    The "Blissful" Approach To Change 54
As Easy As ABC...
    The "Careful" Approach To Change 56
A Good "Game Plan" 59
Change Saves! 61
Whose God Is Too Small?....................63
Extreme Change............................66

Resolving The Palestinian Conflict

Resolving Palestinian Conflict – 10
    Step Plan................................69
Postscript..72

Introduction And Back-story

Most of the pages of this book were written over 10 years ago. The 10 point Palestinian Peace Proposal was offered in the context of knowing how healthy, creative change is achieved. What I propose requires a new way of thinking about how to establish peace. Applying the insights of this short book, a peace process could be initiated and carried out successfully. The most cherished benefits could be attained for all parties.

In order to highlight "A Palestinian Peace Proposal" in 2003, I decided to do a limited edition series of "Essay Art" pieces... to be distributed primarily to family and friends. These were somewhat personal one page sheets... with an "artistic message" computer generated photo on one side... and one step of the Palestinian Peace Proposal on the other. Along with each of the "steps" in the peace process, I wrote a short essay and signed the sheet. The very short essays were intended to briefly develop "the central idea" as well as enable the reader to apply each of the specific actions to daily living. Since significant "change" was encouraged for daily living throughout the series, the Essay Art sheets were extended in number. They concluded with 22 offerings.

So how did all of this begin? Having spent many years studying all the aspects of change I could find, I wanted to pass on (to as many people as possible) the many advantages and benefits of treating change as a "friend". Many people look for improvements in their lives, whether that concerns doing something better or trying to escape something detrimental. Of course, the problem is that we try to avoid change whenever possible because we are such creatures of habit and feel so threatened. In today's ego-centric world the problem is magnified, since we want to assert we are fine as we are and we don't want anyone to tell us how to improve. If we do want to change or to find something different, we want it to come quick, without much effort and without the necessity of facing our "imperfection". So, in a rapidly changing world, we often feel uncomfortable and want more stability. We want to escape and avoid change... so change ends up the "enemy" rather than the "friend". We are caught fighting change but yet needing it to survive.

How does a person get around this dilemma? It can only come in "evolving" just a bit. Everyone faces problems, weaknesses, threats and outright errors in judgment, so most people would grudgingly agree that change is often necessary. Also, if we were to feel more comfortable acknowledging the negatives in our lives, we could more quickly start the process of searching for solutions. We could then open our hearts and minds to deal creatively with the negatives we face

-- admit them, rethink them, adjust them, understand them and so gradually change them. Consequently, at the roots of it all, we really need to understand that we are fallible and frail human beings. We need to always, gradually, honestly be in the process of "change"... if we truly want to live full, rich, productive, happy lives. Looking at change as a friend, every one of us could feel good about maturely moving into a new way of living... plus, feel good about gradually escaping the things that keep us in bondage. Contemplating all this, learning about change as a "friend" and applying all the advantages I had gained in this new friendship

-- all this motivated me to want to share all these benefits... and try to help people get rid of some of their worst terrors. I understood that "the trouble spots" in life are what get people's attention and sometimes motivate them to open up to change. I also knew that no challenge was too great for change. That led me to Palestine.

Who hasn't been troubled by the situation in Palestine? We live in an age where we can hardly avoid hearing all the details of distant discord, destruction and death. Obviously change is needed. But how can peace be established without many people changing? And how can people change if they don't know how? Shall we just wait for a miracle? Will some people need to be "erased" before change comes into view? No, the better solution is to learn how, when and what to change. The better solution is to learn from the world of nature how change is best accomplished. The better solution is to rise up toward an insightful, inspired version of ourselves -- toward goodness, kindness, helpfulness, and insightfulness. Yes, the better solution for Palestine is to simply learn about how to find satisfactory solutions to present problems. But... and this is a very BIG BUT... as time goes on, almost everything changes -- viewpoints, solutions, desires, hurts, fears, hopes, dreams, friends, enemies, leaders, partners, etc. -- everything changes, sometimes for the better, sometimes for the worse. So who will take charge of change? And who will reap the benefits of change? Would you rather have change as a friend or as an enemy? Beneficial change takes time. An extended period of time -- in the ongoing peace process -- will help enable the hopes and dreams of all the parties to be fulfilled.

Is Palestine the center of the world? Could what happens in Palestine be the "blueprint" for how the world looks at how "family relationships" are handled and/or how to work out difficult problems? It could happen... or maybe not. In any case, Palestine is important in the world; it is to me too -- as distant as it might seem. I care about my "neighbors" in Palestine and I want the best for all of them. I want the world to see that people on all sides can find peace in the present and in the future. I want as much peace as possible in a world created "good" and that has so much to offer all its inhabitants. There is enough for all, if we are good caretakers of this planet. Why should I leave Palestine off my list of places where change is appropriate and peace can be accomplished? Why shouldn't an impartial peace initiative come from outside the afflicted nations and peoples? Shouldn't someone with nothing to gain be qualified to make some small suggestions? Why shouldn't a non-politician make a point or two about peace? Trained as a Christian parish pastor, I know a lot about people -- goodness and badness, weaknesses and strengths, hopes and dreams, power and vulnerability, and more. Having been a preacher in the past, I have had some "credentials" to speak up for peace and change. Furthermore, Palestine is the home territory where my Lord grew up. Maybe best of all, I know about agape love and how it works and how it became flesh and what it can do even today. Although I am a "nobody" in political circles, cultural circles, church circles, money circles, theological circles, or any other kinds of circles you can imagine, I can and will speak up for peace... and uplifting, creative and beneficial change. It's a good thing that ordinary people and even "nobodies" speak up for peace, understanding and even cooperation between different people.

Some comments might be helpful concerning "inspirations". As I presented my "Essay Art" pieces, I wanted to relate the peace-making process to daily life, especially since our daily activities are so interwoven with challenging and difficult situations and relationships. People should be able to relate the little details of daily living to the larger field of international relationships. Both have to do with how people interact with one another. In realizing how the personal can relate to the international, individuals can understand how problems and perspectives can be managed with grace and dignity. Mindful of this, with each step of the "peace process" I tried to spell out what the average person could do in daily living to accomplish change and better relationships with the opposition, the "foreigner" and/or as Jesus tried to tell us our "neighbor". "Inspiration for daily living" is intended to make more concrete the approach needed for successful peace-making and to elaborate a bit more deeply what needs to be accomplished. Inspiration" for daily living is meant to be just that -- inspiration (as little as that might be) for living in a little different way -- a more forgiving, uplifting, creative, respectful, helpful, caring and humble way. That's the path to peace for all of us.

Finally, here's what may be "the elephant in the room" -- religion. Many people are inspired by their religious beliefs and are often willing to even die for them. Many people live their lives according to religious traditions and directives... and so are nearly controlled by them. This is not to criticize religions or their beliefs. It's to acknowledge how very powerful religions are in commanding vast populations. When vast numbers of people look at other vast numbers of people as different, even in how they live their lives, big problems can and will arise between those different countries/parties/populations. Evidence of this can be seen in the United States, even between different segments of the same religion -- namely Christians who are "conservative" and those who are "liberal". People on these two different sides can certainly be "miles apart" in their outlooks on life, their politics, their priorities, their religious customs, their ideals and even their interpretations of the Bible. This is a bad, sad problem. Interestingly, our "friend" change has an answer.

It's time, in this 21st century, for religions to "unite".... in order to accomplish real, enduring peace in the world! Yes, that's what I said -- unite -- how crazy is that? If people in our age look at all the various religions of the world, they primarily see differences. Sure, they are easy to see. There are vast differences between religions, and the "critical" people of our world study them and highlight them at every contentious opportunity. That approach is one way to look at religions. But there is another way, and I would assert a better way. Religions, in their most basic tenants, fundamentals, creeds, and beliefs have a lot in common. It's not necessary to point out all the good that religions "proclaim" and urge their followers to support. Basically, we know quite a few of them. Yes, most of us are involved with a particular religion because of it primary, important, motivating good points... not because of the more insignificant things "we don't believe in". But when was the last time you heard people from differing religions talking about the great ideals, concepts or beliefs they share? It almost never happens between "the common people" because they are caught up on all the bad stuff the other people live by. I assert that it's way past time for world religions to start looking at all the good things they have in common and start minimizing (of forgetting about) all the trivia and minor tenants. It would be interesting for people in different religions to see what they share, and furthermore, what they can proclaim as common and basic to human insight.

We would find out that there is much that is worthy of emphasis and is shared by many others. We could begin to see "common ground" and how even this kind of change might create more of the right atmosphere for peaceful living.

Six Principles of Peace

1. It is extremely important for both adversaries to look back honestly at the roots (the history) of the problems between them.

As human beings, we learn a lot about ourselves from history. It teaches us about actions or decisions taken that have produced both good and bad results. Consequently, we can often tailor present actions/decisions to attain what we hope to be a desirable outcome. That does not mean that we can be certain about what will happen in any given situation, since there are often unforeseen factors we may not have considered... which could have influenced the end result. However, we often feel we have a better chance of making intelligent decisions or moves when history is our teacher. Palestine has a lot of history that provides inescapable insights, and it would be foolish not to take a close and extensive look at what has critically impacted a large number of people from many backgrounds.

Even different perspectives on one historical event can be very revealing. A tree can be viewed from different positions and can give interested parties almost totally different "realities" or insights. Getting more than one perspective of any tree is terribly important for a somewhat accurate assessment of what it truly is and how it looks to people. The history of an event isn't much different. Most good historians want to wait quite a number of years to be able to fairly analyze any past event... partly because the event needs to be judged from many angles. Fairness is important for good history and many people appreciate "fairness in life"... as well as in making good, healthy, appropriate, practical decisions.

What then might be the end result of one person inviting another person (looking from a different side of the tree) to come over to "the other side" to take a look? What could be the loss? Or, what might be the advantages? Do you suppose viewpoints could be moderated or maybe even changed from such experiences? The comment about the importance of "walking in another person's shoes" can be somewhat related to this. Most people are quite sensitive to other outlooks and even feelings if they can be drawn in to empathize with another person through some common human experience. Still, this may be the most important factor of all: We have all heard, "The medium is the message!" If the "invitation" is offered in an angry, disrespectful, belittling or haughty "voice", no matter how fair minded the "invitee" might be, there will be little interest in checking out the other side. History is very important, but it also needs to be seen in a somewhat fair-minded context.

2. No lasting peace is possible unless both of the adversaries are interested in resolving "the opposition's" complaints or grievances.

Almost everyone has lost sight of this basic and enduring truth about resolving conflicts. Today, who begins a conversation with an opponent by asking how he or she can make the other person "feel better"? The problem in our "modern world" is that everyone is taught almost from the beginning how to "fight for your rights". We are told that a person can't count on anyone else to look out for one's own interests. So where does that leave us? We are just left "fighting with one another". Obviously, we have plenty of that these days. No wonder conflicts are not easily resolved .

What's the answer? There's really only one. If any conflict is to be truly resolved for the long term, the only way to find enduring happiness and peace is to "make sure the other person (or opponent) is satisfied or content." Now that may take some "sacrifice" and humility, but it's the only way to get the desired results. The consideration that makes this approach tolerable is that both sides need to do the same thing... to the very best of their ability. This is the big "breakthrough" in conflict resolution. Both parties will end up with good results.

To try to make certain the above "answer" is understood and set in motion, consider the impossibility of trying to get "peace" any other way. The human spirit is an awesomely powerful force that usually will not give up, no matter what pressures are applied. Almost everyone (no mater rich or poor, male or female, etc.) will likely go to their death to defend what they believe to be their rightful interests. That's a lot of bloodshed drifting back and forth... over long periods of time. Basically, it's "the law of the jungle" or some might say "the way of the world". The longer people "fight with one another" the more desperate they become... and the further they are from "peace". Who doesn't have some "leverage" or way to make life difficult for the opposition, if they feel they are "pushed into a corner". It's not hard to become a terrorist in today's world. Even "the little animals" can make the world an unhappy place to live.

3. It is critical that as many "influenced people" as possible on both sides have "partnership" or have "a voice" in the peace process.

It's the history of international conflicts that a lot of people have an "interest" in the confrontation. Some may be in large part responsible for bad relationships while others may have been on the receiving end of the sting and hurt of continuing turmoil. Nationalism, intolerance, personal loss, fear, pride, ignorance and even just "feelings" make up some of the barriers that are hard to get around. If these condemnations are not handled or resolved in a fair or reasonable way, it's very hard to satisfy people and keep the peace, as time moves on. People that feel they don't have any part in "peace settlements" can feel justified in "upsetting the apple cart" whenever or wherever they wish... making any peace agreement very tenuous.

Average citizens of countries need to feel important and need to feel understood by their leaders. Leaders need to be "in touch" with the people they represent if they are to be successful and credible. Both leaders and citizens need to work together to implement the many changes necessary for attaining peace, as well as keeping the peace, especially when "conflict" was often the way life in the past. It's much easier to make the necessary mind, body and spirit adjustments if those people have good feelings from having "partnership" in the process.

As more people are involved in the work of finding the path to peace, there is greater momentum to "gaining traction" for peace. Changing a nation's lifestyle is a formidable task and leaders can use as much help as they can get in establishing a united front and a positive spirit. Many people having "partnership" and looking for a better and more peaceful life can take real pride in showing the world what it takes to move toward a better, more healthy, more satisfying, more attractive and more happy life on earth.

4. Beneficial change (in resolving serious disputes) is always done best over a long period of time and therefore needs to be initiated and/or resolved as a "process", not as a "declaration".

It takes quite a bit of time for people to adjust to "new realities" like peace treaties, especially when their whole history as a people has been in enduring a painful and contentious way of life. That's in part why the whole peace "movement" (if in fact there is any "movement") needs to be a process that takes place over a long period of time. Of course, this is exceeding good for everyone involved... if, in the process, there is any movement toward peace. What could be wrong with "something good" growing and developing over many years? People can become accustomed to living in a new way, there is opportunity for creative "gestures" to improve the atmosphere between peoples and new "healthy habits" can be established. Contrast this with "declarations" which... are often the work of a few proud, political people, usually contain a lot of rules and regulations... are quite often imposed on many people, whether they like it or not... and are "made to be broken". On the other hand, a "process" can come from "the grass roots"... makes for active "daily cultivation"... and provides exciting little beneficial "happenings".

But those who uphold "the ways of the world" will not go down without a fight. People who look for a declaration of peace or a treaty or even an arranged compromise are essentially seeking "a quick fix". This is often the desirable solution to many serious problems today. Who wouldn't like to get rid of excess weight, get cured of a serious disease, find the right partner, secure vast riches and live in happiness... simply by finding one quick answer? Our culture has encouraged us to go after "quick fixes" in our fast moving, ego-centric, "have it all now" modern age. Wouldn't it be nice to get those bothersome countries to agree to peace? It would benefit the whole world and we wouldn't need to feel nervous about another dangerous war. So proud, powerful and parading politicians would like nothing better than to arrange an agreement... to secure more prestige and prizes. Does this method work? It hasn't worked for many decades and even for many generations. A new approach is needed -- one that is tested by time, accommodates healthy interpersonal exercises and works to bring many people together for mutual up-building. Who doesn't want to seek after "a more heavenly existence" in the here and now? People are looking for and need an inspired vision for the future.

Finally, if and when a "new vision" is welcomed and "new realities" begin to come into play, it takes time for individuals, communities and nations to change in healthy ways. Large numbers of people need to be involved over exceeding long periods of time for everyone to get into the flow of new circumstances. Some move and change more slowly and others do so a bit faster, but all people need time to heal... and then become better neighbors and friends.

5. "Peace partnerships" (for both of the adversaries) are very important for resolving grievances and for maintaining the peace.

So who doesn't need friends, loved ones, partners, colleagues, and even acquaintances to "keep on top of things", maintain a healthy outlook on life, get good feedback, hear what others are saying and even "get straightened out"? All people do... and so do all representatives in the family of nations. Those who try to "go it alone" usually aren't accepted, become unstable and don't last long. Countries are not much different. They also need help, perspective, encouragement, inspiration and even criticism at times, in order to find health and wholeness. When an individual or nation becomes involved in serious negotiations, it's especially important for that "negotiator" to have "a team" close by. What is exceedingly beneficial in working for peace, is that team members on both sides help moderate things for the benefit of both parties. Imagine the benefits to the peace process if there are representatives from both sides who are "friends" and can find goodness and accommodations for both sides.

Partnerships can serve a number of purposes. Of course, all partnerships are different and all exist at various levels of depth, durability and dependability. That's a good thing, since both individuals and countries need different things at different times and variety is as they say "the spice of life". A partner can supply a sense of security when "challenging events" can be a bit nerve wracking or when there is an underlying feeling of vulnerability. A partner can be reassuring when one gets in trouble. A partner can provide insights from the outside when there don't seem to be any obvious answers. A partner can be present for times of rejoicing as well as for sad and difficult times. There are many things that partners can do, especially when times are tough and one's existence may even seemed threatened. Backup "players" give the whole team a sense of power and stability, which can translate into a more relaxed, self-confident and feel good atmosphere.

It must be emphasized that there needs to be a balance of partnerships on both sides. If the world community of nations really desires peace, then it needs to be active in bringing about "a level playing field". It's a good preparatory exercise for the world community to work for setting up a good negotiating atmosphere -- where there will be perceived fairness as well as understanding of the difficulties for both sides. Interestingly enough, when there is really good competition on both sides of a sports event, and when both sides work equally hard enjoying the competition, and when both teams are well prepared to give their fans the most they can deliver, AND when there is good sportsmanship (applauding the other team's good moves and feeling good when the opposition scores "points") on both sides, then there is a great chance for wonderful advances in negotiations and in the peace process. Yes, setting up good and fair partnership teams plays a large role in accomplishing good, healthy, uplifting long-term results.

6. The work of "establishing/keeping the peace" is never perfectly finished.

Anyone who has had a serious addiction or a long-term bothersome habit to overcome knows that there is almost always the chance of falling back into "the old way of life". Sticking with a program of liberation is essential. The body, mind and spirit does not easily forget (in fact, may never completely forget) what was such normal experience in the past, no matter how long ago and how extreme the negative experience.

Now, multiply that situation by 100 (or whatever) and you will begin to get a feel for what decades of deep resentment and anger... and feelings of vulnerability and helplessness can do within the human spirit. Can this unhealthy state of a human being ever be overcome or given a fresh start? Some would say no, but in any case, the reverse path is a real challenge and a difficult one to travel. One needs the very best of circumstances to find healing and health.

The work of "making peace" is never finished just as the work of "making friends" or "loving someone" is never finished. This is true even before one considers what it means to overcome a great history of terrible, tragic and hurtful events. This is why it is so important that the path to peace is a long-term process. Yes, under even the best circumstances, there will be setbacks. But then the commitment to the long-term goal and hope for a much better life is worth getting back on track and moving forward. No one ever becomes the perfect friend, partner or lover. There is always more to be learned, given and experienced... on both sides.

Can the human mind or spirit yearn for what is perfect? Yes, this is what makes a "yearning for peace" possible and why human beings can attain such awesome levels of caring, sharing, sacrificing, and yes, even changing. The whole world is changing (some might say evolving) day by day, year by year, and human beings are also changing -- for better or worse. Of course, we (as human beings) have a feel for what is better or worse... as well as our impact on the world for what we might consider a quality existence. Will we make the right choices? Will apathy bring us to a dreadful downfall? The winds of time shift and throw us curves that are hard to hit. We strike out, but then we get another opportunity. Has the "game of life" been lost? Have we moved too far into violence, deterioration and death that we cannot find a way out of out deteriorating state? People do die and countries do fall apart for lack of what it takes to change direction to a more creative and redeeming way of living. The path ahead is not easy but it can be traveled successfully. The one thing certain is that the peace process is never finished.

A Letter

The following letter was sent to Prime Minister Ariel Sharon and President Yasser Arafat on March 19, 2003.

Prime Minister Ariel Sharon
Office of the Prime Minister
3, Kaplan Street
Jerusalem, Israel

President Yasser Arafat
The Palestine Liberation Organization
Negotiations Affairs Department
Attn: Director General
P.O. Box 2245
Ramallah, Palestine

Dear President Arafat,
Dear Prime Minister Sharon,

This letter comes to both of you from a citizen of the U.S.A. specializing in "change". We all live in dangerous times and the threats to world peace have been increasing rapidly. Citizens of the United States deserve a good share of blame for the "terror" people feel around the world. We too are people with dreadful power and we cause heartache in many different ways. However, I am a firm believer that "force" will not solve most of the world's conflicts and problems. Although "the stick" is sometimes a necessary motivational tool, very few people are more healthy, happy and content with "more beatings". There is a better way to attain the goals we desire as we enter this new millennium.

Over the next ten months, I am laying out a completely practical and workable ten-step plan as a solution to the Israeli-Palestinian conflict. I have <u>no</u> particular expertise in knowing the feelings and injustices which ravage your area of the world. I <u>can</u> offer you a unique process to attain friendship and mutual support between your peoples. It will not be imposed from the outside. This plan is only offered as an opportunity… to be accepted by both or rejected by either. No pressure to negotiate will be applied from any source. No one but my wife even knows about this letter. I simply have some expertise that I am willing to share quietly. But let me tell you what you have to gain by looking over this unusual, rational, respectful, beneficial and life-changing proposal.

Change is here to stay. We can either control change for the benefit of all people in our world or we can just let change happen according to our "gut instincts". I can assure you with absolute certainty that if there will be a positive future for people on "spaceship earth" over even the next century, "controlling change" will need to be as important to our species as was the industrial revolution or the age of science. Our "gut instincts" will only eventually destroy us and the world that is our home. We can eventually move toward living together in harmony by controlling our appetites and excesses or we can simply go with the flow to our ultimate destruction. "The jungle mentality" will not give many of us even the ability to survive say nothing about peace and happiness.

This is what you as "powerful leaders" have to gain by entering the peace process I propose. First, you will give the peoples you represent hope for guaranteed, concrete gains in the very near future – yes, hope for more than a little peace, meaning and happiness. I would like to think that you both have some good ideas of what a peaceful and harmonious Middle East might be like. Second, you will initiate a process that is able to "turn our world around" as an answer to terrorism and our gradual decline into chaos. For example, citizens of the U.S.A. are presently living in "the dark ages" with regard to our "prison system" and with regard to how controlled, constructive change can take place within the human personality. Then there's our tendency to try to secure what is in our "national interest" through power and force. Personal politics get in the way of wisdom and inspiration. Some generation in the future, if not our own, will hopefully "get it right" about the kind of change necessary to meet the basic needs of all people on our planet. It would be a credit to you and your followers to inspire a changing perspective within the United States. Have you ever heard that comment before? Maybe a better question: Do you think such a proposal is justified and reasonable? Third, and finally, you will obviously be personally strengthened in your leadership as well as admired in history for your wisdom in slowing down the world's march toward self-destruction. Although the least important of the three benefits, this is significant and should be worth a little risk considering the larger picture. The two of you have substantial "influence" in what tools are used to try to attain just and healthy benefits for present and future generations.

I will be releasing my "ten-step solution" over the next ten month period through a series of "Photo Essay Art" pieces – the first enclosed with this letter and entitled "A mazing Change!" This first essay hints at a practical, insightful and beneficial way of looking at "change"... useful for all people. The second piece in this series reveals an attractive, sunset scene from here in Wisconsin and has two titles with the photo – "An Attractive Alternative" and "Go for the Gold!" The first paragraph on the opposite side of this second sheet will dig into "Solving the Palestinian conflict (Step One):" A three sentence paragraph will follow with the simple details that both of you will find interesting and attractive. This second piece will be printed and mailed to only a few family members at the end of March. My method of releasing this "ten-step solution" is as unprecedented and practical as the solution itself. On the chance you are interested in this proposal, I would want to be open to your suggestions about how and when to release each step of the process.

Why should I be interested in your problems a half a world away? As we enter this new millennium, we have become aware that all the peoples of the world are interdependent and created to live on "spaceship earth" in harmony and happiness. The alternative is disaster and destruction for a good share of the world's population in the present and for eventually everyone in the future. That may be "hard to swallow" for leaders presently in conflict. So what does it mean to live without the necessities for happy, peaceful living and without hope for the future? I'm sure you have evidence close to home. We all have choices to make that have implications around the globe and we are extremely naive if we think we can get away with detrimental actions forever... whether we are billionaires or refugees. People pay and the future darkens. The bottom line is that I deeply desire happiness for my "brothers and sisters" in your part of the world, and I would like to offer what I can to help you attain the legitimate desires you have for the people you represent. Frankly, I am extremely happy with my relatively simple and peaceful life and I don't need more work and responsibility. Yet my convictions lead me to simply offer you an opportunity... for endless blessing! My proposal will work and the people of Israel and Palestine will rejoice!

You have no choice but to deal with the realities around you – historically, culturally, politically and personally. I'm certain that life is difficult for you. Whatever choices you and your associates make in the future, I hope those choices will give the people you represent the things they need for quality, peaceful and healthy living – now and in the future. For the sake of our world, we certainly could use evidence from somewhere about how to "change". We all desperately need a much better way of living together.

I do not write this with great pride in our American life-style or aggressive behavior. Please consider me a common friend and an impartial representative of the world community. What I have been given... I am willing to pass on to you as an opportunity for mutually beneficial change. Whatever decisions you make in the coming days, may you both have the inspiration and wisdom to hold out for more than simply the instinct for survival. The history and future of all races and nationalities urge you to strive for "an attractive alternative"!

With concern... and compassion...   T. Hans Olson

A Maze

"Inspiration" for daily living...

A "maze" is a confusing, intricate network of winding pathways. As we enter the 21st century, a few of us may recall some example of a huge, artistic and complicated maze created in a large field or open area. It may have been photographed by airplane or helicopter for publication in a newspaper or magazine. Yet few of us have personally tried to weave our way through such a gigantic intricacy or complexity.

Try to imagine a maze formed on a large field... with walls to the pathways higher than the tallest person. Viewers and visitors soon understand that there is only one entrance and one exit to this gigantic puzzle. Seemingly there are "a million" twisting and turning passageways – some very long, others of medium length and some quite short. There are dead ends to every pathway... all except one! That's the way through the maze to "the other side."

There are several ways to check out a maze. The spectator may contemplate the creation from far above or maybe even from ground level. He or she might marvel at the size, shape and beauty of it all. Of course, the bystander will miss the experience of the maze. On the other hand, the person who enters the labyrinth to find "the way through" is almost immediately caught up in what can become an awesome experience. There's the challenge of the hunt. There's hope for quick success. There's dedication to solving the mystery. Yes, there's excitement, confusion, passion, frustration, anticipation, desperation, anxiety and the magnitude of it all. Finally, the participant in the quest may be able to see the whole adventure as a meaningful, enlightening and enjoyable activity.

A maze highlights change. Healthy change is not only the spice of life and our medium of fulfillment as human beings, but it's also our communion with God. We are uplifted to contemplate that change is exciting movement – venturing away from "the dead end" toward "the life-giving way." What a rewarding, fulfilling and thrilling life-long experience! We can throw ourselves into a mazing change!

An Attractive Alternative

Solving the Palestinian conflict (Step One): There are no preconceived conditions for starting this reconciling process. In the careful and creative search for the solution, the opposing sides will find precisely what they want. They merely enter the unique and rewarding process anticipating huge benefits.

"Inspiration" for daily living...

The first step for finding fulfillment and enduring happiness in life... is recognizing that there is an attractive alternative to normal although regrettable experience. It's not easy to think "outside the box". That's why significant change is so unpopular. People are "creatures of habit" and seem to find satisfaction in ordinary and often troublesome actions. Moreover, it's easy to criticize others and be self-satisfied. On the other hand, conscious, corrective, creative change can take place with special insight and support. There are times in most lives when insight does occur. The moment is often fleeting. Consequently, it's essential to be equipped to handle this grand challenge when it comes. The Lord named "Jesus" knew how hard it would be for the rich man to turn around. Although initially curious, the whole momentum of this man's life held him captive to his old ways. Imagine what might have happened if his "rigid way of life" had been traded in for a new perspective and the tools to venture toward freedom and peace!

Life carries us forward, and we occasionally recognize that there's a dead end ahead! That can give some "liberation" to the egocentric, self-protective, jungle mentality. Buried in a personal crisis, for example, we can get a glimpse of who we are and where we have come from – our imperfections, weaknesses, hurtful actions and destructive tendencies. This can be the start of something special in our lives – something of great significance to accomplish. We can break free of simple survival instincts. We can begin to reach toward our creative potential and our ability to care for the ever changing, creative world that is our home. As we mature and become wise enough to accept great responsibility, we can choose to change and not let pride, independence and selfishness get in the way. In being created for newness we can relish and celebrate true resurrection moment by moment!

The truly blessed person is inspired by the infinitely better way. Such a person is on a mission to "go for the gold"! So change means continuing to look for new opportunities for self-giving, creativity, fulfillment and peace. While the changing person is curious to know what wonderful possibilities might be ahead, God knows there is exciting fulfillment in doing what is especially divine – bringing newness to life!

Back To The Basics

Solving the Palestinian conflict (Step Two): An historical overview of the conflict will be laid out by the best historians from both sides. This "joint report" should include alternating perspectives on each event as each side sees fit. Significant historical events will certainly reveal the origins of battle and bloodshed.

"Inspiration" for daily living...

People willing to study the past and learn from it have a great advantage for making decisions and attaining goals. Since even advanced cultures have not had the ability to predict the future, people have little choice but to look back for answers to "why" and "how" questions. Although history rarely repeats itself, learning from past successes and failures often give individuals and groups insight for future decisions. If there is hope for improved quality of life, a new strategy is often the means to future success.

Studying the past is also extremely helpful for understanding the process of how something takes shape or occurs. We are all products of our past. Watching how past events develop, we become aware that a connected series of occurrences and factors brings about an almost predictable result. The interruption or change of such a process would usually produce a much different outcome. Consequently, in coming to understand how certain events finally happen, people can venture forward with altered actions in confidence that they can change the course of history. They simply use reliable methods to reshape their destinies and so also the destinies of others.

The absolutely glorious benefit in "absorbing the past in order to change the future" is the life-giving power it grants the individual or group. Consider looking back to see a troublesome outcome (an addiction, for example) and then change that limitation with a bold move in a different direction. When a person can see change as a liberating force rather than a threatening one, that individual is in harmony with divine purposes for the world. Imagine all kinds of people looking for new ways to control important change in their lives – the kind of change that benefits the whole creation. Since each part is dependent upon all other parts, each individual is also critically valuable to the health and fitness of the whole. When one entity improves, the whole is raised to a new level of harmonious existence. It's "back to the basics" for power to live in freedom, health, harmony and hope.

Thinking New Thoughts

Solving the Palestinian conflict (Step Three): Representatives of both sides appoint their "best minds" to independently compose a list of

10 things they think <u>the other side</u> wants in resolving the conflict. The requests should be listed 1-10 in order of importance.

"Inspiration" for daily living...

As comfortable as we seem to be with our old habits and interests, almost everyone occasionally desires some newness. Whether it's "a new product" that entices us or "a new way of life," the challenge lies in paying for what we want. What are we willing to offer or sacrifice? Interestingly enough, we are willing to give almost anything if the focus of our desire is big enough. And that's maybe the greatest difficulty. Very few people get much experience creatively contemplating how change can energize and renew their lives – what an awesome benefit change can provide. Consequently, they are usually content with past experience. In the final analysis, change demands not only a price but also a vision of new possibilities.

Today, advertising provides "the vision" that so many people seem to crave with regard to products. We are led to believe that a new deodorant might "turn our world upside down." Here's the maximum payoff for a minimum price... and we are sold! Unlike products which can be easily defined and provide minimum impact on true happiness, new perspective and creative activity are not so easily defined and provide enormous impact on what's important in life. In this area, today's world offers little or nothing to motivate us to get on the right track. Even the promise of heaven doesn't seem to really get people going with the awesome mission of righting the world's wrongs. Sadly, satisfied people are content with the comfortable pew. So we are left with the need for a creative vision of concrete yet infinite possibilities -- vision and hope we can take part in coordinating a better world. "The Spirit" challenges us to take a leap toward newness.

Certainly, there is a cost! Like the leap into the unknown, we leave the comfortable behind and give up a part of ourselves... if not just a part of our past. The cost is... stopping the instinctive habit... being sensitive to a new view... and contemplating fresh possibilities. Put in another way, the sacrifice is... walking in the opponent's shoes... taking in "the enemy"... and going with brains not brawn. Yes, it's brainwashing at its finest... checking out the bigger picture... and figuring we all are family! The price is not too great, however, because of the magnitude of the prize – the destination, the happy new outcome – an enlightened world where cheers come from the other side!

Evaluating Outside Insights Effectively

Solving the Palestinian conflict (Step Four): The lists are switched to be discussed and debated as to the accuracy of the items listed and as to their order of importance.

Requests may be added or subtracted as long as it lists 10 items.

"Inspiration" for daily living...

To reverse direction takes special talent and vision. On the flip side, we have come to learn that going along with the crowd doesn't take much creative insight. "Going along" is as common as mob psychology and following fads. You simply get carried away and pulled down... usually toward trouble and hopelessness. It's true that change sometimes forces itself upon us and we feel violated. But chosen change breaks barriers to meaning, hope, sacrifice and self-giving love. It has led to the greatest inspirations and movements in history. Truly, creative change is something special because it involves the acceptance of personal risk as well as the commendable ability to evaluate outside insights.

It's wonderful that the talent and courage needed for evaluating bold, new ventures is available to everyone. We can be quite certain of this because the key ingredient for picking up new insights is humility, and no one is excluded from holding that character trait. Yet think about how hard it is for some people to really listen to viewpoints from others. What's to gain from an outside perspective? It has been said that there is nothing new under the sun; but certainly there are an infinite number of ways to apply forgotten ideas to new circumstances. The humble insight seekers are the ones who have what it takes to tie everything altogether for significant, creative change.

Obviously each person is limited to a subjective view of what is right or wrong, good or bad, etc. Consider the possible outcome if a person or group did a good job of evaluating and understanding the thinking of the other party. The free flow of information would put participants in the position of knowing the most beneficial and practical approach to any problem. The really gigantic step forward could come when each side in an argument would speak up for the welfare of "the opposition."

Evaluating thoughtful insights from others is a bit like going to the library to do research. It's a privilege and opportunity that can be extremely helpful for finding friendship, happiness, peace, and all we want for the future. Yes, contemplating new ideas for change is the key for opening doors to fabulous success.

Voluntarily Vulnerable

Solving the Palestinian conflict (Step Five): The lists are switched once again to make insightful adjustments... as long as the items remain essentially the same. The ideas are clarified and "embedded".

"Inspiration" for daily living...

The "Teddy Bear" has been one of the most popular, tender and treasured symbols of affection and sentimentality in the past 20th century – especially among Americans. Children, blankets and teddy bears have always seemed to evoke warm and affectionate feelings. All three have exhibited a pleasant and pleasing vulnerability across several generations and many cultures. As it turns out, turning the great, terrifying and ferocious black bear into a child's treasured and lovable "companion" was a stroke of genius. Moreover, even today this transformation symbolizes and provides insight into a life-enhancing benefit for all people everywhere.

It is critical for life on our planet that people can become voluntarily vulnerable – that they can be changed from aggressive, terrifying creatures into caring, affectionate human beings. The greatest of life's intimacies are experienced when individuals and groups can let down their guard and learn how to find closeness with one another.

It would seem that putting your welfare in the hands of your enemy or competitor is the height of foolishness. Yet consider that Saddam Hussain was nearly invulnerable... while seemingly controlled by an evil spirit. Was he to be envied or pitied? The entire history of nature on our planet shows that newness and creativity arise out of the exposed death of the seed. Is The Creator trying to tell us something? To be deeply loved is to be deeply vulnerable. Yes, the infant, lover, sacrificial servant and the apologetic adversary are all adored for their soft spots. After 9-11, millions around the world responded with empathy, care and concern because people had become defenseless and insecure. Shedding power and defensiveness would seem to be a great road map to making up. So how can being critically vulnerable become embedded in us body, mind and spirit?

The answer is a simple matter of choice. We choose to eat or not to eat, to buy or not to buy, to talk or not to talk. So also we choose arrogance or humility, aggression or forgiveness, building up or tearing down. It's simply a matter of choice. The ferocious bear can become the inspiring, embraced and cuddled "Teddy".

Impartial Inspiration

Solving the Palestinian conflict (Step Six): The two lists are brought to an international forum for digestions, discussion and debate… with all the participants offering appropriate help for resolving problems. Each international participant is expected to contribute somewhat equally to both sides.

"Inspiration" for daily living…

We all are taught at an early age to "play fair". Parents who want their children to "get along" help them to learn to take seriously the interests of others. Maybe learning "fairness" is the first step toward understanding "justice" in a civil society. Could it be there is nothing more important for keeping peace in the world than nurturing fairness, impartiality and justice? The concept is so fundamental to stable societies that even religions begin with "divine inspirations" concerning advice about how to get along with others. On the other hand, when people know that they are not treated "fairly", often violence and chaos take root and have a good chance to flourish.

The Olympic games illustrate what may be the world's

best example of harmony and good will between nations, races and cultures. Every four years, the peoples of the world set aside gigantic differences to "play fair". Teams come together in selected cities to celebrate in a "parade of nations" and to promote a special spirit of unity. "The games" accommodate the talents of all races and cultures... with cooperation and courtesy on all levels. Feeling encouragement for great achievements, individuals willingly conform to international standards in order to be able to play and compete at the highest level.

Fairness, inspiration, cooperation and peace -- these weighted words have meaning and practical application in our world today. When a multitude of voices offer their best insights for solving problems between peoples or individuals, creative change has a chance. When people begin to try to look through the eyes of others, their often rigid positions begin to moderate. While walking in the opposition's footsteps of receiving help from an adversary in a time of need, enemies can be turned into friends. As religions so clearly indicate, people look for inspiration and a kind of divine influence upon their lives at critical moments. With such a stimulus to creative thought or action, people can be changed mentally and/or emotionally. In the final analysis, our species "fills the bill" with a broad perspective that helps to encircle what is just and good for all.

Resolving Change

Solving the Palestinian conflict (step Seven): The number 10 issues (for both sides) are laid out on the table to be partially resolved by "the opposition" and the world community. A plan is implemented for the "well being" of the other side. If "the well being" is not accomplished according to independent, impartial, international monitors and according to "the injured party", the plan goes back to step number 6 for discussion and appropriate resolution.

"Inspiration" for daily living...

Positive change is often hard to accomplish. Usually that's because people are "programmed" to simply do what they have always done. However, when an outside force enters the picture, change often happens. The prime example of a parent "inspiring" change in an unruly child is not hard to understand. The "force" changes the programming and something different occurs.

In the case of where all parties are in general agreement that change is desirable, the path to a new way of living is a bit easier to accomplish. Finally, to really get things moving, when "the opposition" is teamed with an all star line-up to make change easy to accomplish, unbelievable progress toward and improved way of living can be implemented. Consider "the force" when a convicted and contrite drug addict finds that the drug dealer, the addict's family, friends, judge and employer are all motivated to see him rehabilitated and get needed help. When the solution doesn't seem to be adequate for healthy, happy rehabilitation, it's back to the drawing board for some new ideas and incentives.

As in nature, change almost never happens in and of itself. In the history of life on our planet, change has almost always happened when the environmental conditions were right. The squeeze of outside factors pushes something new onto the world's stage and opportunity is born. That is not to say that individual people can't have some influence in their future activities. They can see the writing on the wall and conform to the inevitable, or they can resist the tide, sometimes with unbelievable results. However, the most powerful influence comes when all our friends and contemporaries urge us to higher standards than we have previously attained. Change can take place when "the inspiration" is good and powerful and all parties provide incentives for a new way of living. This crucial "encouragement" initiates the process of conforming to the new way. Finally change happens! It's usually just a matter of time.

The Big Picture

Solving the Palestinian conflict (Step eight): Issues 9 to 1 are laid out for resolution in a similar manner to number 10. The added focus on this step is for the international community to begin to sense (or imagine) what "the injured party" might feel is appropriate for resolving the overall conflict.

"Inspiration" for daily living...

Rarely do we take a look at the big picture, when thinking about personal change. We are absorbed with the challenge of doing something different... and we become "near-sighted" rather quickly. Yet in forgetting to look at a bigger perspective, we often lose the chance to take in necessary insights for finally accomplishing what is new and in our best interests. The small child who wants to get his ball on the other side of the street is blind to the perils, pain and penalties of a modern, fast moving world. Similarly, the adult world in its drive for immediate results and self-indulgent satisfaction is careless in a world of environmental consequences, political diversity and religious enthusiasm. Whether we like it or not, we are rapidly coming to realize we live in an interdependent world where every personal action has far-reaching consequences. In the final analysis, life on this planet makes certain that no one gets away with anything!

What is to be gained by widening our horizons when we are struggling with change that challenges us? One important benefit is to learn how the positive change we contemplate will uplift others. It's rather difficult trying to figure out how doing something extraordinary will change our own lives. Of course, that exercise is valuable in itself. However, considering how others might live new and better lives when we alter our actions means that we come to know a whole new "creativity" and power for good. In a very real sense, we extend the beauty and bounty of our world. Furthermore, we inspire our fellow human beings to become more caring for one-another and sensitive to our humble caretaker role in the universe.

One final pitch for looking at the big picture has to do with preserving our world -- our environment. Sadly, today our world is being destroyed by greed, selfishness, violence, killing, racism, nationalism, materialism, terrorism, apathy, arrogance, aggression and pollution -- simple nearsightedness. Yet we know the value of caring for and protecting the greater good. Clearly, to preserve the well-being of "spaceship earth", we need food for the hungry, resources for the needy, representation for the powerless, self-sacrifice for the foreigner, love for the lost, rehabilitation for the convict, and even forgiveness for the terrorist. Rise up... take heart... and look to the big picture for inspiration to change!

The Carrot And The Stick

Solving the Palestinian conflict (Step nine): As issues are being resolved, contributing parties from the international community try to "enhance" the resolution of the previous steps as well as monitor "disruptive elements" in the peace process.

"Inspiration" for daily living...

Most of us have heard about the stubborn donkey that needs motivation to do his work. A carrot is held out to urge him to pull his load and a stick is used to get him going in the right direction. We all are motivated by the carrot and the stick. We all need to be encouraged with rewards and turned away from bad behavior with discipline or correction. Positive and negative stimulation is all we have on this earth to inspire us to attain acceptable and commendable behavior. The difficulty lies in knowing how to use one or both of these tools to produce positive results. In the final analysis, what "works" to bring about desirable change is what needs to be implemented and exercised.

The truth is that imperfect human beings -- individuals, groups and governing bodies -- need both the carrot and the stick in varying degrees in order to attain high goals. Often we as individuals are mistaken about what will bring about good behavior. We persist in applying positive and/or negative stimulation that we think will work but continues to fail. Being creatures of habit, we don't want to give up what we have done in the past, so we press on in our ignorance. As a consequence, often a basic problem even deteriorates as an unproductive stimulus is continued or intensified.

If we want better behavior in the human family, for example, we should begin to implement a change in the application and proportion of positive and negative incentives… toward what brings desired results. It's necessary to explore and initiate creative ideas with differing kinds and degrees of incentives. Often a very different approach may be the answer to a problem that persists or even appears to be getting worse. That understood, we can not be naïve enough to think there will be immediate or unqualified advances. Positive change needs time to take root and grow just as all of nature requires time and influence to bring about change. What's essential is a new process integrated liberally with patience and persistence.

The powerful "force" of people in harmony… working together with truly inspiring stimulation… can cure any problem we face in our world today. Destructive elements cannot prevail against the overwhelming power of positive, persistent change… wisely and creatively contrived using "the carrot and the stick".

The Peaceful Prolonged Process

Solving the Palestinian conflict (Step ten): As the peace process moves forward, both sides understand the natural tendency to slip back into "old habits" that could undermine the positive, prolonged process. Both sides try to do as much as possible to "stay on the wagon" (the need for an AA approach) to benefit both sides. Consultations are arranged between the "peace participants" to work out problems that might arise as well as to solidify friendship and cooperation.

"Inspiration" for daily living...

In our fast moving, impatient age, most of us desire quick and even immediate results. We experience fast food, speedy transportation, prompt entertainment, instantaneous communication, quick retaliation and fleeting relationships. That does not bode well for our long-term happiness on a planet that needs time for goodness to take root and grow. Growing things need extended steps to blossom, mature and produce what is needed on our precious planet. Without growth over time there is nothing but deterioration and death. It becomes obvious that what we desperately need on "spaceship earth" is creativity and change that is integrated with a peaceful prolonged process.

A peace process does not come naturally. What does come naturally, given our instinctive self-centered priorities and desires, is competition, contention, conflict and combat. Individuals, communities, races and governments exist for power and so push to the limits their instincts and boundaries. Mutual destruction is inevitable. A viewpoint born out of education and inspiration... which understands the benefits of the self-giving, sharing and supportive lifestyle... is the only perspective that can provide peace, hope and goodness to all earth's inhabitants and so offer ongoing, abundant living for all people.

Inevitably, individuals as well as governments justify actions that lead to deterioration, destruction and death (physically, mentally and spiritually), or they are inspired toward cooperation, mutual up-building, blessing and goodness for all. The terrible tragedy is that day by day the forces of death and destruction seem to be winning the battle among most of the world's inhabitants. "The movers and shakers" seem caught in instinctive and reactionary blundering that simply increases frustration. The masses follow. Can change come in this repetitive, downward spiral? The answer is, yes.

What is needed is one person of courage in the prolonged process of peace -- one person. One person will hold on with hope. One person will persist with peace. One person will change what needs to be done... for harmony, for friendship and for enduring happiness.

The Beauty Of Change

Solving the Palestinian conflict: The critical perspective There is no hope on earth without change. The status quo simply brings more frustration, destruction and death. The beauty of positive change is that life in the present and future is filled with new possibilities for satisfying and abundant living. Ongoing, self-giving change offers the ultimate yet reachable goal of peaceful, harmonious and meaningful living for all the world's inhabitants. Simply beginning a process of constructive change in solving the Palestinian conflict will inspire individuals and nations to find and apply the critical insights needed to begin to resolve most of the world's problems.

"Inspiration" for daily living…

We have a growing problem of obesity in this country -- the United States of America. Most of us are overweight because we have too much. It's symptomatic of our culture. Some people die of starvation because they have too little. That's not our problem.. We have <u>too much</u>. The only solution to excess weight is to experience a lifestyle change. We need to take in less food and junk… and "work out" more for life and health.

Yes, to make money, advertisers sell us all the "quick fixes" they can imagine... and all the easy solutions we would like to use. But they just won't work, because we still will have too much! There are no easy solutions to our long-term life and health. Moreover, we are called to responsible stewardship of all that we are given. Every thing and every one is precious on "space-ship earth".

It's certain that there are no "quick fixes" to peace in Palestine. In Palestine there is simply <u>too much</u> injustice, hate, destruction and death to solve the conflict quickly or easily... as much s we might desire it. Any solution will take new perspectives, thoughtful gestures, creative problem solving, patient negotiations, realistic goals, heartfelt forgiveness and exciting proposals. There's a lot going wrong in the Middle East and it will take a lot of serious, long-term effort to begin to make it right. Palestine and the Middle East (like many other areas of the world) need "a peaceful process" highlighting tools that will enable change to take root and grow. In fact, there will be no solutions to the Palestinian conflict without the implementation of a "life-style" change.

If there will be a solution to this conflict, sooner or later a process of change will be implemented... not too different from "the ten steps" you have considered. There is no alternative to this kind of change, if we are to witness a vibrant, healthy Palestine. Let's enjoy partnership in this prolonged process -- the beauty of change!

Should We Change?

Learning from Palestine…

"Inspiration" for daily living…

Some of life's changes hit us like a ton of bricks. They are almost more than we can bear! We recoil in horror, anger and frustration. The last thing we want is to be turned away from our normal, comfortable way of life. Although there had always been difficulties in the past, generally, things seemed to be under control. Then suddenly, a major change comes crashing into us. Deep inside, we wonder if our world will collapse around us. In the midst of resistance, we are concerned about how we can deal with the future. We are angry with those who have made life difficult for us.

Are we just stuck with fighting back or could we find another road to travel? There is the possibility of making different choices that might create new opportunities. Now that's not generally a path we want to take. "Choosing to change" involves some new looks… new challenges… new implications… and even new habits. Yet unlike getting hit and hurt by unpredictable change, with desired change we are in control and we can often direct the outcome. That's really important in our world.

Sometimes there are changes that would do everyone some good. Deep inside, you can envision some of those changes. What would make our world a better place in which to live -- a world with less anger, fearfulness, frustration, deterioration, dishonesty, violence, hopelessness, waste, want and uncontrolled speed? There are choices that could help make that happen. Moreover, we could be a part of the choosing and the pace. You know there are actions that just make matters worse. Be certain there are choices that could make things better.

The truth is that we were created for change. We were meant to take part in ongoing newness. That's what religion and faith is all about. The cross was about overpowering our species' less than perfect past and present for faith in a new future. Hope holds out for a more promising tomorrow with a new approach to life -- a kind of daily baptism. If we can change one speck for the better in our little corner of the world, we can have a part in the resurrection and find fulfillment.

If you see an idea you like, pass it on -- make ripples move out over "the pond". Some might call passing it on "a witness" while others might just call it simply "being a friend". Either way, you take charge for a better world. Make a little impact and you can be a lifesaver!

How To Change...

Learning from Palestine...

"Inspirations" for daily living...

Things don't seem to be changing much in Palestine. Of course, there are reasons... and excuses... and ignorance! So why can't we get excited about change? Let's put away the ignorance part. There is relatively easy way to implement controlled change.

The bottom line is that desired change can be accomplished by taking lot of enjoyable "baby steps". Granted, those steps need to be in a new direction -- desirable "brainwashing". The good news is that looking in a new direction doesn't require much more than our natural inclination to survive and a basic desire to improve our lot in life. So let's get the "how to" in front of us.

Here's the "fun part". Using your imagination, pick up a few ideas or tidbits from "a great table-full of appetizing treats". The more pieces you "pick up" and make use of the more empowered you are for success.

Simply pick and choose. The more the better. Satisfy yourself forever!

Write down the reasons why you want to do something different. Likewise, you could also list the reasons you don't like what is hurting you. Refer to these lists often. Those basic exercises will get your mind moving ahead of your body. Maybe you would like to get your spirit involved by rating your desire for change on a scale of 1 to 10. Don't leave out your body. Wouldn't you physically like to treat yourself to a reward for accomplishing that "first step"?

How could you "reverse the process" of having been lured into a bad habit? The secret is to envision how you first got involved... and then to use an opposite strategy to get free. For example, if you started smoking with just one cigarette, start to quit my cutting back just one (over the same period). Keep going and you are in the process of quitting! It's exiting!

Plan to expand your successful change but don't go too fast. Yes, you read that right. It's good to keep the process at a slow pace. By keeping change under control, a person holds on to power, finds gradual, enduring accomplishment and experiences a new pattern for life. All that is much better for meaningful living than an up and down "roller coaster ride"... and it's easy!

See how much fun it would be to ask a friend or loved one to help you to improve your life. Think for a moment what that simple suggestion accomplishes.

Your friend is empowered by providing help while you have initiated a closer relationship. Furthermore, you have support and encouragement to accomplish your goal while also being an inspiration for positive change. Your ability to change will be enhanced as you move forward and your confidence grows. Finally, have a good time experimenting with flexibility. Look for things to change. Run from bad habits! Pray for freedom! Let God guide you! Yes, enjoy the process of finding newness!

Every Cell Has Memory...

Learning from Palestine...

"Inspiration" for daily living...

Let's not blame the Palestinians too much. The peoples on both sides have a lot of history. They also have had a lot of conflict, anger and frustration through many generations. On the other hand, they have also been given the gift of perspective, reason and creativity. There are new possibilities for the future, if they are willing to sacrifice some of their base instincts. Sadly today, few people are willing to follow those who hold out for faith, love and forgiveness. We live in a tough world!

We all have the same options. "The world" would have us believe that it's ridiculous to persist with peaceful and creative programs. Personally, we even yield to the belief that we can't change. There's too much failure and frustration in our lives. So we plod on like the others who complain... and testify to "a lower calling" and "a survival of the fittest". Who will take the risk of change... for a new future... not only for ourselves but also for others who will benefit?

Think about this for living life: Every cell has "memory" -- for good or for bad. Learning the multiplication tables, we went through a lot of memorizing, and finally, little by little, it stuck with us. Suppose you learned incorrect answers from a bad teacher. It would actually be pretty hard to memorize the correct answers to those tables, but it could be done. Generally, it would just take "more conscious effort" to change, the longer you had the incorrect answers stored in your mind. Momentum has a large part to play in our thoughts, words and deeds!

Every cell has "memory". If you ever smoked a cigarette, you probably had a negative reaction the first time. Your body didn't like that "foreign substance" inside your mouth and lungs. It probably remembered and desired relatively clean air. Interesting enough, if you persisted and became "a smoker", your body gradually got used to the idea of having smoke inside -- in fact, every part of you probably wanted it. Although quitting might be difficult, be assured that just as you practiced your way into something bad for your body, you can plan to practice your way out of it. Your physical repetitions and memory push you either way.

Every cell has "memory". Think of the "forces" involved in learning or relearning the multiplication tables as well as in becoming a smoker or quitting an addiction. For wisdom or ignorance, for good or bad, for health or sickness, it was inclinations that moved you further ahead. It was mind, body and spirit as well as your general environment, friends and family that inspired you in your learning. Yet you made the choices. So it is today. What direction are you headed? Don't go so far with what may be bad for you that you have a lot of difficulty going back. Repetitions are crucial for bondage or liberation. Remember, every cell has "memory".

As Easy AS ABC...
The "Artful" Approach
To Change

"Inspirations" for daily living...

Creative "artful change" can be easy. My motto is "Fun change... to easy success". Maybe a bit surprising, change can be as easy as ABC! Let's say that "A" represents the "artful" approach to initiating change. Go ahead and let yourself be a bit creative and artistic as you approach change. Like the child with finger paints and a big piece of white paper, choose your colors, dab in your fingers and start expressing yourself. You will soon find yourself being a bit resourceful, skillful and even "artistic" as you proceed into the process of finding and creating newness.

Look deeply into a 3-D picture. The three dimensions of this picture are Departure, Desire and Destination. All three dimensions are important to the full scope of what change is all about. Putting depth into these three D's will help you to handle change with ease. Now pick out something about your personality or character you've thought of changing. Whether it's big or little doesn't matter. You are having fun here! Once you've decided what you want to change, look at the first dimension -- "departure". What you want to leave behind is what's going to move you forward. Either by yourself or even better with a good friend or two, list three to ten negative things about this bad aspect of your life. When that's accomplished, it becomes obvious you are already making progress. You have a major start on your creative expression.

Next, list three to ten positive things about your "destination" -- the goal you'd like to reach. Consider your life on the other side of change. People who go on vacation can almost taste what it will be like to arrive at a refreshing, special place. Because of their plans and anticipation, chances are they will be happy, excited and fulfilled. What new activities will be able to be accomplished? How fast will the days go by? Will there be any special surprises along the way? Will the new environment be comfortable? The whole venture could be very exciting and a life changing experience.

Finally, think about how enthusiastic you are to make this change and rank your "desire" from zero to ten. This is where it gets real personal. You lay yourself on the line here. Maybe you are as high as a kite. Or it's possible you are not ready for newness. Maybe something will come along to increase your desire. In any case, don't worry about it. Your desire is an expression of your inner self in the present moment. Realize that even if you have little desire to change, you can still manage to accomplish it.

Each of these 3-Ds can be increased with greater outside inputs or perspectives. You now have an "artistic" 3-D image of where you are going with change. Put on your 3-D glasses to look into your motivation to escape from your old place... to go to your new destination. Have fun!

As Easy As ABC... The "Blissful" Approach To Change

"Inspirations" for daily living...

Being successful at change can be fun and even easy... as easy as ABC. The "artful" approach to initiating change can get us started on accomplishing commendable goals. We simply need to let our creative talents help us <u>depart</u> from regrettable activities and move us toward fascinating <u>destinations</u> we greatly <u>desire</u> for the enhancement of our lives. All this happens in a world of people, where "the good life' is directly related to our connections with others. Social creatures that we are, family and friends can even give us inspiration for living. Certain relationships are deep and meaningful... and some can be eve 'blissful" -- full of great joy and happiness. Our second "blissful" approach to change is dependent upon at least one great relationship -- one where the long-term welfare of the other person is exceedingly important.

Personal change in people's lives can be wonderful, rewarding experiences, especially when change can be accomplished between two friends at the same time. Obviously, every person has flaws and weaknesses. Imagine two individuals who both understand and acknowledge at least one of the other's weaknesses. How easy it would be for each to agree to encourage and support the other in escaping that certain flaw or hurtful habit. The rewards could be tremendous.

A mutually supporting or "blissful approach" requires a vision for what is better -- what makes a person become more satisfied, healthy, successful, confident, insightful and productive. It means enjoying a process of helping raise the friend to a more meaningful and wonderful life. Who else would be better qualified to monitor or encourage progress? Can one imagine friends not wanting to get together... or not wanting to talk about their problems... or not wanting to help one another? There's true joy in the other's company and in bringing about long-term happiness. Spending time to help develop a friend's "untapped treasure" is satisfying indeed.

Teams share goals and inspire one another. Friends can do the same. Great goals are needed for change. For accomplishing change, people need to get inspired or "fired up"

-- maybe like feeling the joy and excitement of falling in love. Friends can provide such ingredients to achieve exciting, meaningful and shared victory. It's not strange that interdependent relationships provide enduring hope for people everywhere. The difficulties of change get lost in a blissful, long-term process. Someone has said, "A friend in need is a friend indeed".

As Easy As ABC... The "Careful" Approach To Change

"Inspirations" for daily living...

Advantageous change is easy, if a person can understand and apply certain fundamental principles to daily life. It's clear that analyzing the past and contemplating the future can help to start one down the road toward desired change. Furthermore, using human creativity and close relationships to support efforts toward life enhancing change can greatly increase the probability of success. Yes, the "artful" and "blissful" approaches are very helpful to people who strive for accomplishment and expanding happiness.

The "careful" approach to change is probably the easiest to learn. Personal change is important to someone who acknowledges "making a wrong turn" and "traveling down a wrong road" in life. Who hasn't headed off in a wrong direction? The "trick" is in getting turned around... or even better, just heading off in a little different direction. Usually, however, there's little or no awareness of how it all started. For example, bad habits usually begin very innocently -- with one cigarette, a beer at a party, stealing a small item, a one night stand, etc. Innocently, "just one" leads to another... and another... until a person is maybe psychologically and physically caught in a web of confusion, frustration and misery. The same thing can happen with personality traits or physical conditions. When a person is on one of those roads to nowhere, there's not much satisfaction just continuing to feel lost. The only rational decision is to acknowledge the wrong turn and head off in a different direction.

Personal change is the adventure of moving toward a better destination. An individual caught in the addiction of smoking, for example, probably will find it easier to escape in the same way he or she got drawn in. Put yourself in the place of a smoker who uses 50 cigarettes weekly. The body adjusted to the slow increase over time. Likewise, the body (and mind) will "adjust the easiest" with a slow decrease over time. The whole creation since the beginning has made "corrections" in this manner. It's the little things that count. So count the total cigarettes you smoke in one week. Then start subtracting one each week until you quit. It's simple... and easy to accomplish.

With any change, recognize the importance of body, mind and spirit. All three should be in tune with seeking the little changes and reaching your goal. As you head out in a new direction, encourage your body and all your senses with kindness, fortify your mind with knowledge, truth and virtue, and inspire your spirit with beauty, goodness and divine insights. Finding success, you will also be preparing for a great future.

A Good "Game Plan"

"Inspirations" for daily living...

The competition always seems to get better. That's particularly true in most sports, but it also seems to be true with regard to getting into college, finding a good job, winning over customers, clients and converts or succeeding in relationships. Generally, a person needs to be really good at something to be truly successful. Practically from the time we are born, our ambitious culture encourages us to do our best... to survive, if not get ahead.

In sports today, most of us are aware of the strategies of success. Coaches and managers carry out a lot of analysis to find the slightest weaknesses of their teams. They attempt to turn deficiencies into strengths with good planning. Since the competition is so intense, they know if they don't earnestly attempt to overcome their "problem areas" and inadequacies they will lose their chance for pride and popularity.

As unique individuals, we also feel the need to do things well. All the way from succeeding with baby steps to landing an adult leadership position -- nearly every accomplishment enhances our self-esteem. As we mature, we begin to realize that just doing what comes naturally doesn't always help us reach our goals. In fact, just letting change happen almost certainly get us into trouble because we have little control over the way things turn out. Those who take charge and change their bad habits with insight, courage, creativity and power are equipped with the intangibles for ongoing success.

Defensiveness about personal change can really hurt us in the long run. Sadly, sometimes we feel the need to defend our right to do it "the old way" -- the way we've always done it. We lose in more ways than one in those cases, when we are almost certainly wrong. Usually we have just unconsciously slipped into unhealthy patterns that eventually will guarantee failure. However, since our egos seem to be more powerful than our better judgment we continue to slide toward inadequacy and disaster. When we begin to mature and study new strategies for success, we will want to go about initiating the changes that eventually will make us successful.

It's not very hard to take up the challenge to look at what we do in a new and better light. Most of us basically already know a good "game plan". The key is to implement that plan in our daily activities so that we can develop the skills to make controlled change a reality in our lives.

Change Saves!

"Inspirations" for daily living...

Generally, we are quite aware of what takes us down. Terrorists took down the twin towers along with a lot of America's loved ones. That hit us like a ton of bricks. Obviously, destroyers also include street drugs, lost jobs, poor family relationships, the slumping economy, bad study habits and the list goes on. Finally, we are drawn into a lot of bad choices and unusual circumstances that make life hard. Sometimes difficult problems and traumatic events just keep getting to us until we can't take it anymore.

Are there any answers? Bumper stickers and signboards say, "Jesus Saves!" A lot of advertising also attempts to get us to imagine what might solve our problems. Much money is made with diet plans, entertainment devices and get rich schemes... along with products promising to make us more attractive, powerful and popular. It's not so strange people hurting and under pressure desperately look for ways to find freedom from their troubles and hope for the future. Sadly, a lot of "easy answers" just don't work!

Change saves! Think about it. When we slide into bad

habits, poor priorities, hurtful relationships, ignorant choices or immoral activities, we honestly could look ourselves in the mirror and head off in a different direction. Of course, finding a better way presupposes we have the courage and knowledge to deal with change creatively. Christians know Jesus requires change and better choices in order for people to find abundant life. Of course, not every person Jesus faced wanted to change. A lot of people are pretty defensive about their bad choices and egocentric rights. So they resist "the change that saves" and lose out on one of the most rewarding and exciting adventures human beings can ever experience.

Getting it right with change does awesome things for body, mind and spirit -- for the whole person. Who doesn't like humility, creativity, leadership, morality, discipline, courage, adaptability, intelligence faith, hope and love in another person? Those are qualities usually evident in someone who can handle change effectively. Moreover, every human being is perfectly suited for change because we know that absolute perfection is unattainable. Imagine a world comfortable with healthy change.

Doing it differently is being able to adapt. We know the whole creation has been in the process of adapting since the very beginning. In fact, anything that doesn't change for a higher standard or adapt to "the way of life" is ruined. Certainly individual happiness and our species' future depend upon appropriate change. So for everyone's sake, make "change that saves" one of your life enhancing priorities.

Whose God Is Too Small?

"Inspirations" for daily living...

There are lot of pretty small gods in today's world. As in Old testament times, individuals, communities and even nations want to fashion expedient gods -- pretty gods, personal gods, convenient gods, controllable gods. But they all turn out to be exceedingly small. From ancient Israel's golden calf, down through the ages and into today's church buildings, people like to build false gods to enhance personal pleasure. There's lots of misplaced faith, personal prayer requests, feel good adoration, big egos and lost souls. Dealing with the snake... or the devil, pious and religious people take great pleasure in being able to judge good and evil as well as establish self-serving, justifiable, pretentious rules for pious, self-centered living.

On the other hand, contemplate the Christian God... in the person of Jesus Christ. The Christ represents the god of the few and far between. This Lord commends servant-hood ... love of enemies... sacrifice for the sake of the world's poor and powerless... the justice worship of freeing prisoners and forgiving debt... even turning the tables and bringing down the rich and powerful of the world. Of course, that's a god "unheard of" in our capitalistic culture of power politics and immediate gratification. We seek retribution while He seeks forgiveness. We strive to justify ourselves while He strives to humble himself. We want to lead while He looks for followers. Here's a god almost beyond our comprehension. So where can we locate One who will get us through the turmoil of the present and future?

We need significant change in our politics and lifestyle these days. God is betrayed by the kiss of war, greed, self-righteousness, egocentric leadership, blind nationalism, personal religion and entertaining worship. The gods of revenge, killing, force, power, nationalism, wealth and ego are mighty small; yet they are forever the same in honoring death and destruction. On the other hand, the Christian God blesses change and honors new life. We are called to worship the creator God who owns it all, who calls individuals and nations to be His caretakers, who challenges the rich and aids the poor, who wants all His children to live in peace and love of one another, who wants to win hearts and minds through love and sacrifice, and who offers abundant life to those willing to change direction. There is a wrong and right way to live. The right way is inspired by the Good News of agape love and faithfulness to a heavenly vision of God's world.

Life-giving healthy change can inspire us to bless others with whatever they need for meaningful living.

Being grounded in "The Word made flesh", we will not be tormented to hear, "Your god is too small!" Our mission will be to "give legs" to a vital way of living and turn the heads of the multitudes toward "the One above all others".

Extreme Change

"Inspirations" for daily living...

Everyone needs change for life in our world. We are dependent on nature's ebb and flow for healthy living. Maybe even more important than learning to be comfortable with the changes around us and within us is the ability to handle "extreme change". Being "in tune" with our source of life, our inner selves, our environment and our destination is important to a fulfilling and thankful lifestyle. On the other hand, being "out of tune" with these elements can get us into trouble very fast. Extremes upset and corrupt the delicate balance of life. Not only do the extremes get the whole world into trouble but they can send our personal lives into chaos as well.

Great spiritual truth warns us about the extremes. The Christian faith and the Bible (from Genesis to Revelation) guide our species into right relationships -- with God, with our environment and with one another. An extreme in even one aspect of our lives (no matter which end of the extreme we are on) can "upset the apple cart", so to speak. Human beings need to be cautious about moving toward extremes and are wise to liberate themselves from them whenever they have the opportunity.

Think about the extremes that are causing serious trouble today. One of the greatest extremes is the gap between the rich and the poor. Jesus Christ was deeply concerned about this one, but in recent centuries the separation has grown much worse. Which person is to be pitied more -- the irresponsible lottery winner or the terribly poor person? Then there are the extremes between freedom and bondage, force and apathy, perfection and corruptness, security and insecurity, a big ego and low self esteem, meticulousness and sloppiness, over eating and starving -- the list can go on and on. Multiply the imbalance in one person with the world's population... and humanity's future is in real danger.

What we desperately need as we enter the 21st century is "extreme" change. One of the best phrases to advance abundant life for all people is, "Love your neighbor as yourself!" The phrase does not say "more than" or "less than" but "as" yourself! Consider what our world would be like if everyone was equally loved and nurtured. Yet too many desire extreme luxury, padded pews, the best medical care and perfect products. You get the point. We destroy ourselves and put others in jeopardy when we are at the extremes. On the other hand, the path to abundant life for our planet is for satisfied and thankful people to seek moderation through humble sacrifice and generous love. Handling extreme change, we need to reject the argument, advertising and preaching that caters to greed, power grabs and destructive tendencies. We need to be good and healthy!

Enough is enough! Cutting back on our extremes leaves opportunity and hope for others.

In doing that we will find lasting peace.

Resolving Palestinian Conflict – 10 Step Plan

Solving the Palestinian conflict (Step One): There are no preconceived conditions for starting this reconciling process. In the careful and creative search for the solution, the opposing sides will find precisely what they want. They merely enter the unique and rewarding process anticipating huge benefits.

Solving the Palestinian conflict (Step Two): An historical overview of the conflict will be laid out by the best historians from both sides. This "joint report" should include alternating perspectives on each event as each side sees fit. Significant historical events will certainly reveal the origins of battle and bloodshed.

Solving the Palestinian conflict (Step Three): Representatives of both sides appoint their "best minds" to independently compose a list of 10 things they think <u>the other side</u> wants in resolving the conflict. The requests should be listed 1-10 in order of importance.

Solving the Palestinian conflict (Step Four): **The lists are switched to be discussed**
and debated as to the accuracy of the items listed and as to their order of importance.

Requests may be added or subtracted as long as it lists 10 items.

Solving the Palestinian conflict (Step Five): The lists are switched once again to make insightful adjustments... as long as the items remain essentially the same. The ideas are clarified and "embedded".

Solving the Palestinian conflict (Step Six): The two lists are brought to an international forum for digestion, discussion and debate... with all the participants offering appropriate help for resolving problems. Each international participant is expected to contribute somewhat equally to both sides.

Solving the Palestinian conflict (step Seven): The number 10 issues (for both sides) are laid out on the table to be partially resolved by "the opposition" and the world community. A plan is implemented for the "well being" of the other side. If "the well being" is not accomplished according to independent, impartial, international monitors and according to "the injured party", the plan goes back to step number 6 for discussion and appropriate resolution.

Solving the Palestinian conflict (Step eight): Issues 9 to 1 are laid out for resolution in a similar manner to number 10. The added focus on this step is for the international community to begin to sense (or imagine) what "the injured party" might feel is appropriate for resolving the overall conflict.

Solving the Palestinian conflict (Step nine): As issues are being resolved, contributing parties from the international community try to "enhance" the resolution of the previous steps as well as monitor "disruptive elements" in the peace process.

Solving the Palestinian conflict (Step ten): As the peace process moves forward, both sides understand the natural tendency to slip back into "old habits" that could undermine the positive, prolonged process. Both sides try to do as much as possible to "stay on the wagon" (the need for an AA approach) to benefit both sides. Consultations are arranged between the "peace participants" to work out problems that might arise as well as to solidify friendship and cooperation.

Postscript

How does peace-making get started or begin to gain traction in a world seemingly headed in the opposite direction? There's no question that the most important initiative has to come from "the little people" who have lived in "the battle field". When those people begin to "see the light" and even begin to act differently, then there is real verification that the peace process is moving forward. Here are a number of words and actions that almost anyone can accomplish. These are not small things that are trivial or without importance. They are the "real deal" day by day activities that make ripples flow outward and change the world. Could you imagine yourself accomplishing one or more activities like these?

1. Talk to your family and friends about your desire for peace and how it can be accomplished in the here and now.

2. Use the "social media" (Face book, Twitter, etc.) to make peaceful, influential comments for all to see.

3. Use your presence at work or at school to be a visual symbol of peace... and of openness to change.

4. In any way possible, support those who are peace-makers and work for a new outlook among members of your community.

5. Think up a little "action of peace" or signal to the opposition that you want to be friends and improve relationships.

6. Withdraw support for people who want to be "fighters" or who want to instigate anger and retaliation.

7. Be obvious in applauding people who speak up for peace and change… so that your leadership will influence and move others.

8. Change your troublesome feelings, attitude or viewpoint even a little bit. How? First, by simply being a good actor. The "acting" will be easier as time goes on.

9. Seek out knowledge and insight concerning "the opposition's" position on one or more important current events.

10. Let your creativity loose to come up with a new idea that would promote peace and help people to live in harmony with one another.

11. Let your imagination run wild in dreaming up a future of ongoing peace-making and radically improved relationships.

12. When the opportunity presents itself, take a little personal risk for peace or for showing friendship to some part of the opposition.

13. Begin to look at yourself as a "peace-maker"... or as a person who has changed your position for the sake of a better world.

14. Write a sentence, paragraph or article about the benefits of the peace process and publicize it to the best of your ability.

15. Organize a "peace party" where the only contribution to the happiness of all attendees is in offering an idea for a change that just might work.

16. Send a card or letter to a leader you admire and express your interest in compromise and accommodation for the sake of people on the other side.

There are many more. Only you can imagine them. The peace process is in motion.

Go in peace!

www.ingramcontent.com/pod-product-compliance
Lightning Source LLC
Chambersburg PA
CBHW020514030426
42337CB00011B/378